BAROQUE TO MODERN

Upper Elementary Level

32 Pieces by 16 Composers in Progressive Order

T0081815

Compiled and Edited by Richard Walters

On the cover:
Detail from *The Rainbow Landscape* (1636–37)
by Peter Paul Rubens (1577–1640)

Detail from *Landscape with Cows, Sailing Boat and Figures* (1914)
by August Macke (1887–1927)

ISBN 978-1-4950-8860-5

G. SCHIRMER, Inc.

DISTRIBUTED BY

HAL•LEONARD®

7777 W. BLUEMOUND RD. P.O. BOX 13819 MILWAUKEE, WI 53213

www.musicsalesclassical.com
www.halleonard.com

CONTENTS

Though the table of contents appears in alphabetical order
by composer, the music in this book is in progressive order.

iv **COMPOSER BIOGRAPHIES, HISTORICAL NOTES and
PRACTICE AND PERFORMANCE TIPS**

Johann Sebastian Bach
16 "Air on the G String"
    from Orchestral Suite No. 3 in D Major, BWV 1068

Béla Bartók
12 Walking from *The First Term at the Piano*

Ludwig van Beethoven
23 Ecossaise in G Major, WoO 23

Mélanie Bonis
    Selections from *Album pour les tout-petits*, Op. 103
40   The Sewing Machine (La machine a courde) (No. 6)
36   Meow! Purr! (Miaou! Ronron!) (No. 15)

Johann Friedrich Burgmüller
32 Arabesque (L'arabesque) from *25 Easy and Progressive Studies*, Op. 100, No. 2

Norman Dello Joio
5   Mountain Melody from *Suite for the Young*

David Diamond
15 Pease-Porridge Hot from *Eight Piano Pieces*

William Duncombe
18 The Chase

Morton Gould
26 Loud and Soft from *Ten for Deborah*

Cornelius Gurlitt
28 Morning Prayer (Morgengebet) from *Albumleaves for the Young*, Op. 101, No. 2

    Selections from *The First Lessons*, Op. 117
7   Vivace (No. 8)
2   To School (Zur Schule) (No. 14)
4   Cradle Song (Wiegenliedchen) (No. 17)

Dmitri Kabalevsky

Selections from *24 Pieces for Children*, Op. 39

8   Waltz in D minor (No. 13)

3   Jumping (No. 15)

39   Clowns (No. 20)

Selections from *35 Easy Pieces*, Op. 89

37   The Shrew (No. 12)

19   Little Goat Limping (No. 19)

11   The Little Harpist (No. 24)

13   Stubborn Little Brother (No. 27)

Wolfgang Amadeus Mozart

10   Minuet in C Major, K. 6 (I)

22   Minuet in B-flat Major, K. 15pp

21   Air in A-flat Major, K. Anh. 109b, No. 8 (15ff)

Jean-Philippe Rameau

6   Menuet en Rondeau (Minuet in the form of a Rondo)

Robert Schumann

Selections from *Album for the Young*, Op. 68

38   Melody (Melodie) (No. 1)

29   Soldiers' March (Soldatenmarsch) (No. 2)

Dmitri Shostakovich

Selections from *Children's Notebook for Piano*, Op. 69

24   The Bear (No. 3)

34   Merry Tale (No. 4)

30   Sad Tale (No. 5)

Charles Henry Wilton

20   Amabile from Sonatina in C Major

9   Minuet from Sonatina in C Major

COMPOSER BIOGRAPHIES, HISTORICAL NOTES

AND

PRACTICE AND PERFORMANCE TIPS

JOHANN SEBASTIAN BACH
(1685–1750, German)

One of the greatest composers in the history of music, J. S. Bach defined the high Baroque style, developing counterpoint in composition further than any composer before him or since. However, during his lifetime he was more known for his virtuoso organ and harpsichord playing than for composition. Relatively few people were familiar with the works of J.S. Bach in the decades after his death. The modern wide recognition of Bach as a master composer began in the mid-nineteenth century, decades after his death, first championed by Felix Mendelssohn. Throughout his life Bach wrote keyboard music for his students, including his children. Bach composed hundreds of works, most for practical occasions, including cantatas, oratorios, motets, various instrumental suites, harpsichord works, organ works, and orchestral pieces. He came from a long line of musicians, and was father to six noted composers.

"Air on the G String"
from Orchestral Suite No. 3 in D Major, BWV 1068
This air is the second of five movements in this famous suite, composed around 1730. The entire suite is for trumpet, oboe, timpani, strings and basso continuo, but the second movement is for strings and continuo only. It was a 19th century arrangement by violinist August Wilhelmj of the second movement, transposed so that the entire melody can be played on the lowest string of the violin, that became known as "Air on the G String," and that nickname has stuck since. Bach's original music is in D Major, transposed to C Major in Wilhelmj's version, and also in C Major for the arrangement in this collection.

Practice and Performance Tips
- Tempo must be absolutely steady throughout.
- The hands play with different articulation throughout. The right hand plays a *legato* melody. The left hand plays detached notes, but not short *staccato*.
- The constant quarter notes of the left hand need to be very evenly played, with the same duration and tone. Practice this separately.
- Practice the right-hand melody alone, aiming for smoothness and expressive phrasing.
- To get a sense of the piece, it would be helpful to listen to a recording of the original orchestra composition for inspiration.
- Use no sustaining pedal.

BÉLA BARTÓK
(1881–1945, Hungarian;
became a US citizen in 1945)

Béla Bartók is one of the most important and often performed composers of the twentieth century, and much of his music, including *Concerto for Orchestra*, his concertos, his string quartets, and his opera *Bluebeard's Castle*, holds a venerable position in the classical repertoire. His parents were amateur musicians who nurtured their young son with exposure to dance music, drumming, and piano lessons. In 1899 he started piano and composition studies at the Academy of Music in Budapest and not long after graduation he joined the Academy's piano faculty. Bartók wished to create music that was truly Hungarian at its core, a desire that sparked his deep interest in folk music. His work collecting and studying folksongs from around the Baltic region impacted his own compositional style greatly in terms of rhythm, mood, and texture. Bartók utilized folk influences to create a truly unique style. Though he composed opera, concertos, ballets, and chamber music, he was also committed to music education and composed several piano works for students, including his method *Mikrokosmos*. Bartók toured extensively in the 1920s and '30s, and became as well-known as both a pianist and composer. He immigrated to the US in 1940 to escape war and political turmoil in Europe, and settled in New York City, though the last years of his life were difficult, with many health problems.

Walking from *The First Term at the Piano*
With the original Hungarian title *Kezdõk zongoramuzsikája*, these short pieces were selected from the 44 pieces Bartók composed for a piano method by Bartók and Sándor Reschofsky, published in 1913. The pieces were composed for piano students at Reschofsky's music school in Budapest. Some of the pieces are based on folksongs, others are original compositions. Fingerings, articulation and metronomic markings are by Bartók. The little pieces in *The First Term at the Piano* were the great composer's only compositions in 1913.

Practice and Performance Tips
- In giving right and left hands different dynamics, the composer is encouraging independence of the hands.
- Practice each hand separately at first, playing the dynamic as composed.
- Playing the left hand *f* and the right hand *p*, then switching (in measure 5) requires coordination and concentration. This will take quite a bit of practice for most students.
- Notice from the phrase markings that the entire piece is played smoothly, no matter whether *f* or *p*.
- Keep a steady tempo, in the spirit of the even stride of walking.
- Do not use pedal.

LUDWIG VAN BEETHOVEN
(1770–1827, German)

Beethoven was the major figure of the transition from the Classical Era to the Romantic Era in music. As one of the first successful freelance composers, as opposed to a composer thriving in a royal court appointment, Beethoven wrote widely in nearly every genre of his day, with emphasis on instrumental music. He acquired wealth and fame beyond any composer before him. Beethoven's chamber music, piano sonatas, concertos, and symphonies are part of the ever-present international repertoire. In his youth he was regarded as one of the greatest pianists of his time, but he stopped performing after hearing loss set in. He devoted an enormous amount of his compositional efforts to the piano, which as an instrument came of age during his lifetime. He was occasionally a piano teacher, with wealthy patrons and young prodigies begging for lessons, though this task was not a match for his nature. However, teaching piano did inspire him to write many pieces for students. Because his piano music is so widely spread across the level of difficulty from easy to virtuosic, Beethoven's piano music is played by students and professional pianists.

Ecossaise in G Major, WoO 23
An ecossaise was a fast tempo European dance of the 18th and 19th centuries. This Ecossaise was originally written for military band, transcribed for piano by Carl Czerny.

Practice and Performance Tips
- Like all dance music, the tempo should be kept very steady.
- Begin practice hands separately at a slow tempo; then hands together at a slow tempo.
- Only increase the tempo when you have mastered the music.
- Learn the articulations from the beginning as you are learning the notes.
- Learn the *p* section by playing at *mf*, then when comfortable try it at a soft volume, but without loss of tone or tempo.

MÉLANIE BONIS
(1858–1937, French)

Because women were not taken seriously as composers in the 19th century, Mélanie Bonis used the male pen name Mel Bonis. Though she showed extraordinary talent, her working class Parisian family was opposed to her musical study. César Franck taught her as a teenager and through him she enrolled in the Paris Conservatoire, studying piano, harmony and composition, and winning prizes. Her parents were against her romance with a singer, and forced her to marry a well-off man 25 years older than she. Her husband and children showed no interest in her music. In the 1890s she had an affair with the singer she had fallen in love with at the Conservatoire years before, and secretly had an illegitimate child she could not acknowledge for many years. Bonis became a member of the French composer's society, including being recognized as a remarkable talent by elite composers of the day, such as Saint-Saëns. In the first decade of the 20th century her music had some public performances. She suffered from poor health in her last years, but continued composing. Bonis was extraordinarily driven as a composer, writing on her own without hearing her music. She wrote over 300 works of chamber music, art song, choral music, orchestral pieces, and piano music. Only a few compositions were published in her lifetime, and included *Album pour les tout-petits* (Album for the Little Ones), Op. 103, composed in 1913.

The Sewing Machine (La machine a courde) from *Album pour les tout-petits*, Op. 103, No. 6
Practice and Performance Tips
- This short little, happy piece has a few technical challenges.
- The pattern of D-E on staccato quarter notes in the left hand throughout must be played perfectly evenly. This will take practice. This is the hum on the sewing machine.
- The right-hand melody shows the happiness of the seamstress at her task.
- In measures 11–18 the left hand is above the right hand.
- In measures 20 and 22 to the end, the right hand crosses over the left hand.
- Practice can begin slowly, at *mf*, before achieving the tempo and then backing down to a controlled *p*.

Meow! Purr! (Miaou! Ronron!) from *Album pour les tout-petits*, Op. 103, No. 15
Practice and Performance Tips
- Imagine a kitten gently walking on the piano keys.
- Don't try to play softly until you have mastered the piece. At that point, observe *pppp*, which is the composer's way of saying, "play as softly as possible."
- There are musical challenges, such as measure 13, where the composer asks for a swell of volume and a slowing down, followed by a return to the opening tempo and a sudden shift to *p* on the downbeat of measure 14.
- The composer's indication of *lié* at the opening means linked, and probably implies using sustaining pedal.

JOHANN FRIEDRICH BURGMÜLLER
(1806–1874, German/French)

The Burgmüllers were a musical family. Johann August Franz, the patriarch, was a composer and theatre music director as well as the founder of the Lower Rhine Music Festival. Johann Friedrich's brother Norbert was a child prodigy at the piano and a composer. Johann Freidrich distinguished himself from his family by leaving Germany and establishing a career in Parisian circles as a composer of French salon music. Later in life he withdrew from performing and focused on teaching. He wrote many short character pieces for his students as etudes. Several collections of these are perennial favorites of piano teachers, especially opuses 100, 105, and 109.

Arabesque (L'arabesque) from *25 Easy and Progressive Studies*, Op. 100, No. 2
Practice and Performance Tips
- It can be tricky to find the right tempo and maintain it steadily throughout this piece.
- In a fast tempo piece, choose the most difficult spot. How fast you can play that is how fast you can play the whole piece. You can't slow down for hard spots.
- For most players, the left-hand sixteenth notes in measures 12–17 will be the most difficult spot. Make sure you don't slow down in this section.
- Begin practice at a slow tempo, hands separately.
- Be sure to observe all *staccato* markings.
- Use no sustaining pedal.

NORMAN DELLO JOIO
(1913–2008, American)

One of the most notable American composers in mid-20th century, Norman Dello Joio grew up in a musical home in New York City, the son of an Italian immigrant father who worked as an organist, pianist, singer, and vocal coach. Musicians were constantly in the home, including singers from the Metropolitan Opera who came for coaching sessions. Dello Joio worked as an organist in his teens, before deciding to turn his attention to composition instead. After initial composition study at the Institute of Musical Art and The Juilliard School, he began studying with Paul Hindemith at the Yale School of Music. Hindemith encouraged Dello Joio to embrace the natural tonal lyricism of his writing (as opposed to the atonality then in vogue), which was infused with the spirit of Italian opera and the church music of his childhood, as well as early jazz. Dello Joio remained true to his style in writing operas, ballets, orchestra pieces, solo instrumental works, art songs, piano music, and choral music. He was on the faculties of Sarah Lawrence College, the Mannes College of Music, and Boston University.

Mountain Melody from *Suite for the Young*

Suite for the Young (1964) is the only music for piano Dello Joio wrote for the first or second year piano student.

Practice and Performance Tips
- The piece has the feel of a simple folk tune, made interesting by Dello Joio's harmonization.
- Notice the indication *legato*, and the composer's phrase markings.
- The melody begins in the right hand, then is almost exactly repeated an octave lower in the left hand.
- Note the rather dramatic dynamic changes, including the sudden shift to *mf* in measures 5 and 8.
- Even with the strong dynamic contrasts, this piece needs to be played with a gentleness of spirit.
- Use no pedal. Create the smoothness of this music with the fingers only.
- A slight *rit.* is possible in the last two measures.

DAVID DIAMOND
(1915–2005, American)

David Diamond was born in Rochester, NY, to Austrian and Polish parents. He studied at the Cleveland Institute of Music and the Eastman School of Music, then with Roger Sessions at the New School in New York before traveling to Paris to study with Nadia Boulanger. A Guggenheim Fellowship allowed him to remain in Paris until the outbreak of World War II. Diamond and the neo-classicists held a different view from the atonalists in fashion in mid-century. Although the upward trajectory of his career tapered off, he remained part of the New York scene. From 1973–1986 he was professor of composition at The Juilliard School of Music. He continued to teach there following his retirement until 1997. Interest in his works revived in the 1980s and 1990s when he won the Gold Medal of the American Academy of Arts and Letters, an Edward MacDowell Medal in 1991, and President Bill Clinton's National Medal of Arts in 1995. Diamond wrote two piano sonatas, two piano sonatinas, five preludes and fugue for piano, and a few other works for the instrument.

Pease-Porridge Hot from *Eight Piano Pieces*

Eight Piano Pieces (1940) were inspired by nursery rhymes, children's songs, and other images from childhood.

Practice and Performance Tips
- Diamond's short piece has the spirit of a modal old English tune.
- The challenge to the progressing pianist is the multi-note chords.
- Highlight the contrast between the legato phrase in measures 1–2, 5–6, 9–10 with the chords in measures 3–4 and 7–8.
- Play the chords marked with a *tenuto* (–) with slight separation.
- The most complex spot is measure 12, when notes are added to the chords. A *rallentando* helps to make this ending both graceful and powerful.
- No pedal is recommended until measures 11–12.

WILLIAM DUNCOMBE
(1736–1818 or 19, British)

Very little is known about the life of Duncombe. He served as the organist in the London district of Kensington. Apart from the handful of short pedagogical works, such as the Sonatina in C Major and an often heard fanfare, his music is now virtually unknown.

The Chase
Practice and Performance Tips
- Music inspired by hunting horn calls is common in the 18th and 19th centuries.
- Begin practice hands separately and slowly.
- Prepare for the change of hand position in the left hand, moving from measure 8 to 9.
- Practicing C-major arpeggios in both hands would help master this piece.
- The most challenging section for most will be measures 9–11, where the hands are close together.
- Use no sustaining pedal.

MORTON GOULD
(1913–1996, American)

Morton Gould was born in Queens to an Australian father and a Russian mother. He composed his first work, a waltz for piano, when he was six. At eight he entered the Institute of Musical Art, which would later become The Juilliard School. His first work was published by G. Schirmer in

1932 when he was eighteen. Gould was a distinctly American presence, writing in both popular and contemporary classical styles and proving himself adept at conquering the rising mediums of radio and cinema. For radio he composed commercial jingles and radio symphonettes, and he also worked as a conductor, arranger, and composer for WOR New York's weekly "Music for Today" program. In 1933, Stokowski premiered his *Chorale and Fugue in Jazz* with the Philadelphia Orchestra. Gould wrote in various styles and blurred the lines between classical and popular music. Besides concert works he also wrote for Broadway. His works were performed by the New York Philharmonic, the Cleveland Orchestra, and other leading orchestras. In 1994 he was awarded a Kennedy Center Honor for his contributions to American culture, and in 1995 he won the Pulitzer Prize for his final orchestral work, *Stringmusic*, which he wrote on commission for the National Symphony Orchestra as a farewell to Mstislav Rostropovich.

Loud and Soft from *Ten for Deborah*

Ten for Deborah (1964) was written for Gould's daughter while she studied piano.

Practice and Performance Tips
- The 7/4 measure is divided in to 4 beats + 3 beats throughout, indicated with a dotted bar line.
- Articulation has been carefully composed, with staccato markings, slurs, accents and pedaling.
- Learn the articulation as you learn the notes and rhythms, not added later.
- Practice should begin at a slow tempo. Gradually increase the speed as you master the music, but always keep a steady beat, whatever the tempo.
- Use pedal only in the places Gould has composed, and only exactly as indicated.
- It is very important to point up the sharp contrasts in dynamics, especially in a piece titled "Loud and Soft!"

CORNELIUS GURLITT
(1820–1901, German)

Many of Gurlitt's piano works have colorful, descriptive names, which is no surprise given his lifelong interest in art. He studied music in Leipzig, Copenhagen, and Rome, where he was nominated an honorary member of the papal academy Di Santa Cecilia. His brother Louis was a very successful artist in Rome, and Cornelius himself studied painting for a time while living there.

Gurlitt worked as a pianist and church organist, and also served as a military band master. He returned to his hometown of Altona, where the Duke of Augustenburg hired him as music teacher for three of his daughters. Gurlitt wrote symphonies, songs, operas, and cantatas, but he is best remembered today for his pedagogical keyboard pieces.

Morning Prayer (Morgengebet)
from *Albumleaves for the Young,* Op. 101, No. 2
Practice and Performance Tips
- This music has the character of choral singing, or organ playing.
- Practice hands separately first. In your practice attempt to achieve *legato* with the fingers only and without pedal.
- When practicing hands together, make sure all notes of a chord are struck exactly together.
- When you add sustaining pedal, listen very carefully to keep the changes of harmony clear.

Vivace from *The First Lessons,* Op. 117, No. 8
Practice and Performance Tips
- Begin practice slowly, hands separately.
- In the right hand, the notes not marked by slurs should be played slightly detached, but not short *staccato*.
- After you master the right hand, increase your practice speed until you can play the piece fast and evenly.

To School (Zur Schule)
from *The First Lessons,* Op. 117, No. 14
Practice and Performance Tips
- This little pieces features scale work. Your practice of scales will pay off!
- The eighth notes need to be evenly played throughout, in either hand.
- Practice the hands separately.
- Notice the quarter note rests in the left hand in measures 2, 4 and 12.
- Gurlitt has given quite specific dynamics for this short student piece. These will bring the music to life.
- Use no sustaining pedal.

Cradle Song (Wiegenliedchen)
from *The First Lessons,* Op. 117, No. 17
Practice and Performance Tips
- Practice hands separately.
- It is most important in playing the left-hand accompaniment that it be steady, even and flowing.
- The right-hand melody should expressively "sing" above the left-hand accompaniment.

- If need be, practice can begin at *mf*. Once the piece becomes comfortable, play softly, in the spirit of a lullaby.

DMITRI KABALEVSKY
(1904–1987, Russian)

Kabalevsky was an important Russian composer of the Soviet era who wrote music in many genres, including four symphonies, a handful of operas, theatre and film scores, patriotic music, choral music, vocal music, and numerous piano works. He embraced the Soviet notion of socialist realism in art, a fact that was politically advantageous to his career in the USSR. While studying piano and composition at the Moscow Conservatory, he taught piano lessons at a music college and it was for these students that he began writing works for young players. In 1932 he started teaching at the Moscow Conservatory, earning the title of professor in 1939. He eventually went on to develop programs for the concert hall, radio, and television aimed at teaching children about classical music. In the last decades of his life, Kabalevsky focused on developing music curricula for schools, retiring from the Moscow Conservatory to teach in public schools where he could test his theories and the effectiveness of his syllabi. This he considered his true life's work, and his pedagogical principles revolutionized music education in Russia. A collection of his writings on music education was published in English in 1988 as *Music and Education: A Composer Writes About Musical Education.*

Selections from *24 Pieces for Children*, Op. 39
Kabalevsky began writing piano music for students as early as 1927. His first major set, *30 Children's Pieces*, Op. 27, was composed in 1937–38. *24 Pieces for Children* (alternately titled *24 Easy Pieces*), Op. 39, for an earlier level of study than Op. 27, was composed in 1944. Though Kabalevsky composed operas, orchestral music, concertos and chamber music throughout his career, as well as more difficult piano literature, he returned to writing music for piano students periodically in his life, reflecting his deeply felt commitment to music education.

Waltz in D minor (No. 13)
Practice and Performance Tips
- Throughout the right hand plays a melody, accompanied by the left hand.
- Practice the right hand alone to create a beautiful and flowing melody, playing smoothly, noticing the composer's phrasing.
- If played without phrase structure, this melody will not be what Kabalevsky composed.
- Also practice the left hand separately, keeping this simple accompaniment gentle and quiet.
- With hands together, let the melody in the right hand be slightly louder than the accompaniment in the left hand.
- Play this lovely, melancholy waltz with no pedal.

Jumping (No. 15)
Practice and Performance Tips
- The piece is almost hands in octaves throughout, but with the composer's brilliant and simple twist of delaying the first beat in one hand by half a beat.
- The left hand leads in measures 1–8 and measures 17–23. The right hand leads in measures 9–16.
- The trickiest spot is measure 9, when the lead switches to the right hand.
- The articulation is key to successfully playing "Jumping."
- Throughout, the notes of beat 1 are slurred to a *staccato* note on beat 2, followed by a *staccato* note on beat 3.
- Note the sudden change to *p* in measure 9, followed the *crescendo* beginning in measure 15.
- The tempo and the title of the piece are clear indications of its fun spirit.
- Use no pedal at all.

Clowns (No. 20)
Practice and Performance Tips
- Begin practice hands separately and slowly.
- Learn the articulation (slurs, *staccato*, accents) as you learn the notes and rhythms.
- Learning the articulation from the beginning will help you learn the notes and rhythms.
- The melody is in the right hand, played with slight prominence over the left hand.
- The left-hand *staccato* notes should be played with a light bounce.
- Exactly and crisply playing the slurs, staccato, accents and dynamics will convey the fun shenanigans of circus clowns.
- Use no pedal at all.

Selections from *35 Easy Pieces*, Op. 89
Kabalevsky's last large set of piano pieces for students was composed between 1972–74 when the composer was in his late sixties, after a lifetime of experiences with young musicians, and after he had attained a revered position as the cultural leader of music education in the USSR. These were

also his last compositions for piano. After 1974 Kabalevsky only wrote a few more compositions, which were songs or small choral pieces.

The Shrew (No. 12)
Practice and Performance Tips
- Kabalevsky is teaching the student about the enharmonic spelling of notes in this piece.
- An enharmonic note means that the same pitch is notated different ways. For instance: B-flat or A-sharp.
- Left and right hands play the same notes in octaves throughout.
- Most measures are comprised of an accented half note slurred to a short eighth note.
- Learn and accomplish the articulation with the fingers only before using the pedaling Kabalevsky has composed.
- When using the pedaling, be sure to release exactly as you play the eighth note on beat 3.
- This is a character piece, in this case a portrait of a strident, hot tempered woman (a shrew).

Little Goat Limping (No. 19)
Practice and Performance Tips
- For this piece in 5/4, the composer has helped by putting in dotted bar lines to divide the measure into two groups: 3 beats + 2 beats.
- Find the natural lilt in this music in 5/4, with a stronger emphasis on beat 1, followed by a lighter emphasis on beat 4.
- Executing the slurs and accents as Kabalevsky composed them will create the character of the piece.
- We suggest playing beats 3 and 5 in the right hand in measures 1–3 with separation just short of true *staccato*.
- Notice how the composer decorates the melody a bit when the music from measures 1–4 returns in measures 9–12, with different slurring the second time.
- Use no pedal in this crisply rhythmic piece.

The Little Harpist (No. 24)
Practice and Performance Tips
- As the title indicates, this music imitates a harp.
- It is crucial to play the composer's phrasing, passing the phrase from hand to hand.
- A traditional technical approach would be to practice slowly, deliberately playing *non legato*, making each sixteenth note very even.
- Follow the above by playing smoothly and elegantly, but attempting to retain the evenness of the sixteenth notes.
- As the music is mastered, the tempo can increase.

- Practice without pedal. Kabalevsky (who often indicated pedaling in his piano music) did not mark any pedaling, a strong clue that he intended this little piece to be played without pedal.

Stubborn Little Brother (No. 27)
Practice and Performance Tips
- The wit of this adorable piece comes from someone attempting to persuade sweetly, with a blunt response that refuses to comply.
- Through most of the piece (except for measures 18–20) the right hand plays smoothly and the left hand plays with strong *marcato* accents.
- Practice slowly hands together.
- The pedaling is by the composer. Pedal exactly as he wrote it, using pedal nowhere else.
- Be sure to release the pedal cleanly, exactly in the spot the composer indicates.
- Typical of Kabalevsky, the piece has many intricate details of articulation, slurring, dynamics and pedaling, all composed along with the notes.

WOLFGANG AMADEUS MOZART
(1756–1791, Austrian)

One of the most astonishing talents in the history of music, Mozart was first a child prodigy as a composer, keyboard player and violinist. He developed into one of the greatest composers who has ever lived, with a vast output in opera, symphonies, choral music, keyboard music, and chamber music, all accomplished before his death at the young age of 35. Mozart spent most of his adult life living and working in Vienna. He was at the end of the era when successful musicians and composers attained substantial royal court appointments. A major position of this sort eluded him, despite his enormous talent, and he constantly sought opportunities to compose and perform. His music embodies the eighteenth century "age of reason" in its refined qualities, but adds playfulness, earnestness, sophistication and a deep sense of melody and harmony. Mozart's piano sonatas, concertos, sets of variations, and many other pieces at all levels from quite easy to virtuosic have become standards in the literature. His first compositions as a boy, from age five, were for keyboard. The notes on the individual pieces below were adapted from material previously published in *Mozart: 15 Easy Piano Pieces* (Schirmer Performance Editions).

Minuet in C Major, K. 6 (I)
This minuet was first published in February 1764 (Mozart was eight years old) in Paris as Op. 1, No. 1.

Practice and Performance Tips
- Practice to achieve the fluent gracefulness and clarity that the music requires.
- In this period composers indicated few articulations. We have made bracketed editorial suggestions to help achieve the style.
- In this edition we have recommended how the appoggiaturas in measures 8 and 16 can be interpreted.
- It might help to imagine a violin playing the right hand melody, and a cello playing the left hand music.

Minuet in B-flat Major, K. 15pp
Practice and Performance Tips
- The opening motive of the falling octave is followed by a gracefully lyric phrase.
- Articulation is crucial in bringing this dance music to life. This edition makes stylistic suggestions for playing a minuet of the 18th century with period style.
- Create strong contrasts between staccato notes and the slurred notes.
- Mozart's music asks for perfection in playing. Any flaws are very noticeable.
- It will take quite a bit of practice to achieve a fluent, elegant performance.

Air in A-flat Major, K. Anh. 109b, No. 8 (15ff)
Practice and Performance Tips
- As with all Mozart, this music requires an even touch.
- Play with smooth *legato* throughout.
- In this period composers indicated few articulations. We have made bracketed editorial suggestions to help achieve the style.
- At this Andante tempo, with the gentle mood of the music, trills should be played at a slower speed than in quicker music.
- Practice can begin at a louder dynamic. After mastering the music, try for beautiful tone at a soft volume.
- Aim for clarity and elegance. Use no sustaining pedal.

JEAN-PHILIPPE RAMEAU
(1683–1764, French)

Rameau studied with his father, an organist, before continuing his music education in Italy. He returned to France as a violinist in a traveling music troupe and then became organist at Clermont Cathedral. By 1706, Rameau was in Paris serving in various places as organist and publishing his first keyboard works. After a few brief appointments as organist in Dijon and Lyons, Rameau returned to Paris permanently. He published his most famous theoretical work, *Traité de l'harmonie*, in 1722. Late in life, the composer took up writing operas. Rameau is remembered as one of the most influential composers of keyboard music of the French Baroque.

Menuet en Rondeau
(Minuet in the form of a Rondo)
Practice and Performance Tips
- First, as with all music, practice slowly.
- In music inspired by dance, such as a minuet (menuet is the French spelling), it is most important to keep a very steady beat.
- Practice the right-hand flowing eighth notes separately, playing evenly and gracefully.
- The left-hand quarter notes should be slightly detached, but not short *staccato*.
- Use no sustaining pedal.

ROBERT SCHUMANN
(1810–1856, German)

One of the principal composers of the Romantic era, Robert Schumann's relatively short creative career gave the world major repertoire in symphonies, art song, chamber music, and piano music. Besides being a composer, Schumann was an accomplished writer about music, especially as a critic, then editor of the influential *Neue Zeitschrift für Musik*. He was married to concert pianist Clara Wieck, who championed his works after his death, the result a severe struggle with mental illness. Schumann was an early supporter of the young Johannes Brahms. *Album for the Young* (*Album für die Jugend*), a collection of 43 short piano pieces, was composed in 1838 for Schumann's three daughters. Schumann made a specialty of short character pieces for piano, not entirely unrelated to his distinctive work as a major composer of art song.

Melody (Melodie)
from *Album for the Young*, Op. 68, No. 1
Practice and Performance Tips
- Schumann gave no tempo for this piece, so it's open to interpretation. There needs to a flow to the moving eighth notes of the left hand, but it shouldn't be too fast either. We recommend a tempo somewhere between quarter note = 100 to 116.
- Practice hands separately. Aim to play the left hand with a fluid, even sound.

- The left hand is an accompaniment to the melody in the right hand. The right-hand melody should be beautifully phrased and have a singing quality about it, like a vocal melody.
- The < > indication in measures 5–7 and 13–15 show that the marked melody notes should be stressed by slightly extending them. They are not to be louder, but expressive, as if a singer were slightly holding out a vowel of a word in an expressive way. It will take some practice to get the feel for this.

Soldiers' March (Soldatenmarsch)
from *Album for the Young,* Op. 68, No. 2
Practice and Performance Tips
- Begin practice hands separately, slowly. Then hands together slowly.
- Only increase the tempo when you have mastered the music.
- Notice the sustained quarter notes of measures 17–18, 21–22, and 29–31. Make sure these are played correctly, distinguishing them from the eighth-note/eighth-rest pattern.
- There is a tendency to play the eighth notes followed by eighth rests (such as in measures 2–4) as *staccato.* If Schumann had wanted true staccato, he would have marked it so.
- Practice very slowly and count each eighth note of the measure: 1-AND-1-AND. Release the eighth-note chord exactly on the eighth rest that follows it. Listen carefully. Increase the tempo, staying aware of how long you are holding the eighth-note chord and when you are releasing it.
- Use no sustaining pedal.

DMITRI SHOSTAKOVICH
(1906–1975, Russian)

A major mid-20th century composer, Shostakovich is famous for his epic symphonies, concertos, operas, string quartets, and other chamber works. Born in St. Petersburg, his entire career took place in Soviet-era Russia. His life teetered between receiving high official honors and living with an almost debilitating fear of arrest for works that did not adhere to the Soviet ideals of socialist realism. In 1934, his opera *Lady Macbeth of the Mtsensk District* met with great popular success, but was banned by Stalin for the next thirty years as modernist, surrealist, and obscene. The following year, Stalin began a campaign known as the Purges, executing or exiling to prison camps politicians, intellectuals, and artists. Shostakovich managed to avoid such a fate, and despite an atmosphere of anxiety and repression,

was able to compose an astounding number of works with originality, humor, and emotional power. He succeeded in striking a balance between modernism and tradition that continues to make his music accessible to a broad audience. An excellent pianist, Shostakovich performed concertos by Mozart, Prokofiev, and Tchaikovsky early in his career, but after 1930 limited himself to performing his own works and some chamber music. He taught instrumentation and composition at the Leningrad Conservatory from 1937–1968, with brief breaks due to war and other political disruptions, and at the Moscow Conservatory in the 1940s. Since his death in 1975, Shostakovich has become one of the most-performed 20th century composers.

Selections from *Children's Notebook for Piano,* Op. 69
Among a huge output of symphonies, operas and chamber music, Shostakovich wrote only a few pieces for piano students. *Children's Notebook for Piano* was written for his eight-year old daughter, Galina, for her studies on the instrument in 1944. The original set was published as six pieces. The seventh piece, "Birthday," written for Galina's ninth birthday in 1945, was added in a later edition.

The Bear (No. 3)
Practice and Performance Tips
- This light-hearted, comical piece seems to capture a bear at mischievous play, or maybe a circus bear.
- Practice hands separately first.
- The *f* sections should have a buoyant touch, even though playing loudly.
- Make the most of the sudden changes from *f* to *p* and back to *f.*
- Any sustaining pedal would spoil the crisp rhythm of this piece. Use no pedal at all.

Merry Tale (No. 4)
Practice and Performance Tips
- Practice hands separately, first at a slow tempo.
- Learn the composer's articulations (*staccato,* slurs) from the beginning, not added later.
- In measures 1–3 in the right hand, make a distinction between the *staccato* eighth notes and the non-accented quarter notes.
- After hands-alone practice, move to slow practice with hands together, retaining the articulation you have already learned.
- In this piece there are several 4-bar phrases that sound similar but have subtle differences. Compare measures 1–4, 9–12, and 33–36, as well as measures 17–20 and 25–28.

- This piece needs a crisp, light touch, even in *f* sections.
- Any sustaining pedal would completely spoil the texture of the music. Use no pedal.

Sad Tale (No. 5)

Practice and Performance Tips

- The composer's marking of *legato sempre* indicates that the entire piece should be played smoothly.
- Begin practice slowly, hands separately.
- Strive for an evenness in tone in smoothly moving from note to note, without the help of the pedal.
- Measure 13 is a classic Shostakovich key change. Make it special!
- Feel the richness of the low range starting at measure 50. Imagine this as a passage scored for cellos and basses in one of Shostakovich's symphonies.

CHARLES HENRY WILTON
(1761–1832, English)

Not much is known about Wilton. He studied violin in his hometown of Gloucester, and continued study in Italy. He was active on the London musical scene as orchestra leader and singer. Later in life he settled in Liverpool as a piano teacher, and composed music for students. Date of composition of the Sonatina in C Major is unknown.

Amabile from Sonatina in C Major

Practice and Performance Tips

- Begin by practicing hands separately.
- Pay careful attention to fingering in the moving thirds of measure 4.
- Notice in the left hand how in measures 1 and 3 there are quarter notes, followed by quarter rests, contrasted with half notes in measure 2. Do not play measures 1–3 the same.
- Pay careful attention to the recommended articulations, contrasting the slurred sixteenth notes with the *staccato* eight notes in the right hand.
- The quarter notes of the left hand, such as measures 5–7, could stylistically be played slightly detached.
- *Amabile* means likable or lovable. The music needs a friendly good will in performance.

Minuet from Sonatina in C Major

Practice and Performance Tips

- Begin by practicing hands separately.
- The right hand needs to be played with flowing, graceful motion.
- Play the short two-note slurs in the left hand with a slight lift after the second note that does not disrupt the tempo.
- The quarter-note chords on beats 2 and 3 in measures 7 and 15 can be played with slight separation, but not true *staccato*.
- Keep a steady beat. Remember that a minuet is a graceful, courtly dance.

— Richard Walters, editor

These pieces were previously published in the following
Schirmer Performance Editions volumes.

Bartók: Walking from *The First Term at the Piano*
Dello Joio: Mountain Melody from *Suite for the Young*
Diamond: Pease-Porridge Hot from *Eight Piano Pieces*
Gould: Loud and Soft from *Ten for Deborah*
from *The 20th Century: Upper Elementary Level*
edited by Richard Walters

Ecossaise in G Major, WoO 23
from *Beethoven: Selected Piano Works*
edited by Matthew Edwards

Arabesque (L'arabesque)
from *Burgmüller: 25 Progressive Studies, Op. 100*
edited by Margaret Otwell

Morning Prayer (Morgengebet)
from *Gurlitt: Albumleaves for the Young, Op. 101*
edited by Margaret Otwell

Waltz in D minor
Jumping
Clowns
from *Kabalevsky: 24 Pieces for Children, Op. 39*
edited by Margaret Otwell

The Shrew
Little Goat Limping
The Little Harpist
Stubborn Little Brother
from *Kabalevsky: 35 Easy Pieces, Op. 89*
edited by Richard Walters

Minuet in C Major, K. 6 (I)
Minuet in B-flat Major, K. 15pp
Air in A-flat Major, K. Anh. 109b, No. 8 (15ff)
from *Mozart: 15 Easy Pieces*
edited by Elena Abend

Melody (Melodie)
Soldiers' March (Soldatenmarsch)
from *Schumann: Selections from Album for the Young, Op. 68*
edited by Jennifer Linn

The Bear
Merry Tale
Sad Tale
from *Shostakovich: Children's Notebook for Piano, Op. 69*
edited by Richard Walters

To School
(Zur Schule)
from *The First Lessons*

Cornelius Gurlitt
Op. 117, No. 14

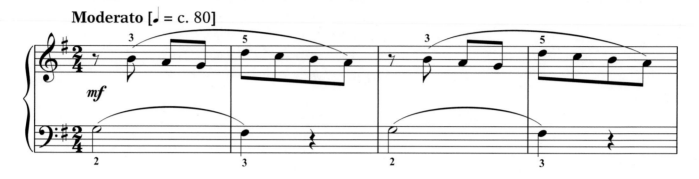

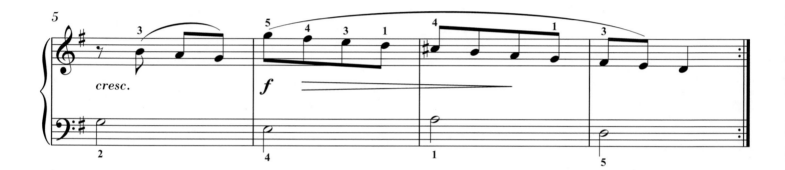

Fingerings are editorial suggestions.

Jumping
from *24 Pieces for Children*

Dmitri Kabalevsky
Op. 39, No. 15

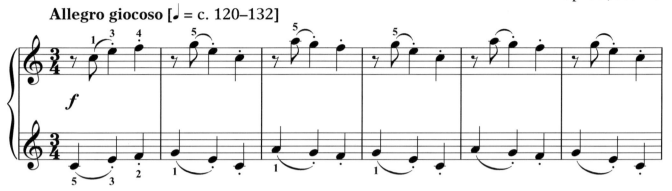

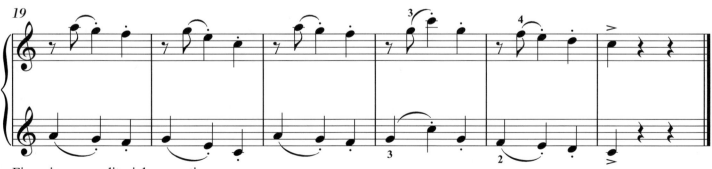

Fingerings are editorial suggestions.

Cradle Song
(Wiegenliedchen)
from *The First Lessons*

Cornelius Gurlitt
Op. 117, No. 17

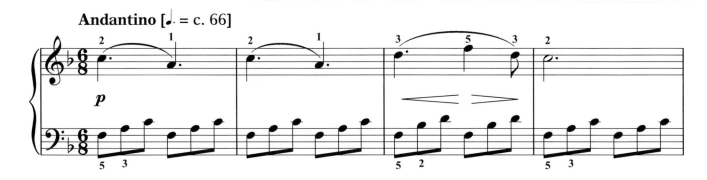

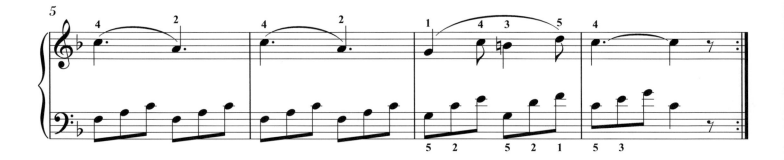

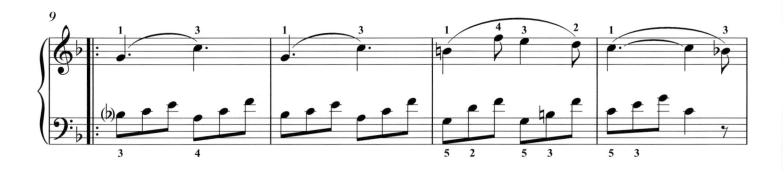

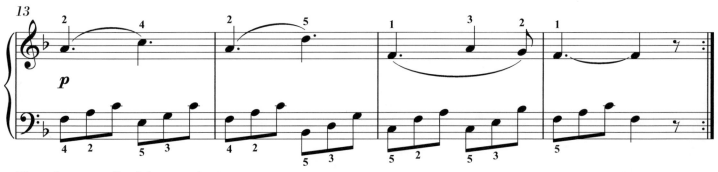

Fingerings are editorial suggestions.

Mountain Melody
from *Suite for the Young*

Norman Dello Joio

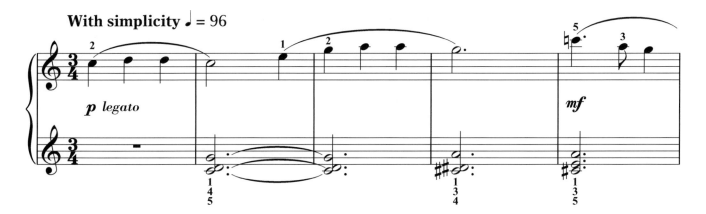

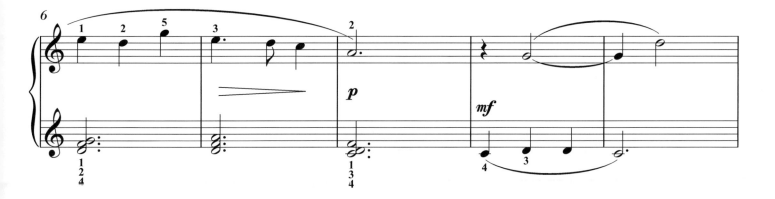

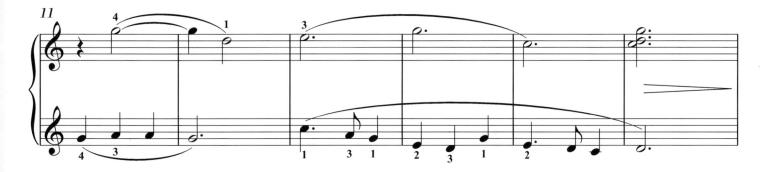

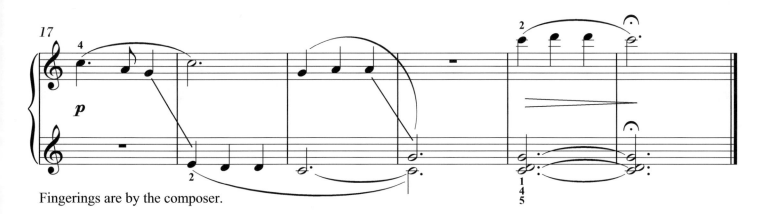

Fingerings are by the composer.

Menuet en Rondeau
(Minuet in the form of a Rondo)

Jean-Philippe Rameau

Allegretto [♩ = c. 128]

Play quarter notes slightly detached throughout.

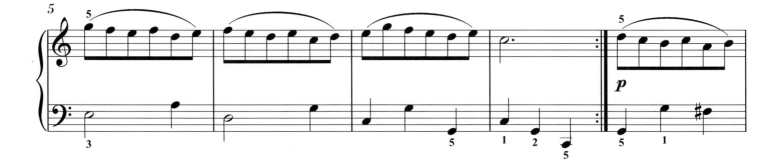

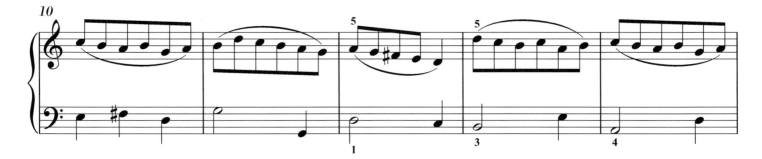

Dynamics, fingerings, and articulations are editorial suggestions.

Vivace
from *The First Lessons*

Cornelius Gurlitt
Op. 117, No. 8

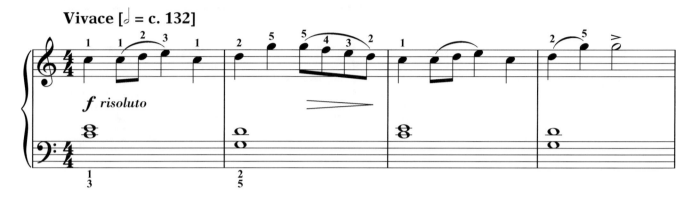

Fingerings are by the composer.

Waltz in D minor
from *24 Pieces for Children*

Dmitri Kabalevsky
Op. 39, No. 13

Moderato [♩ = c. 104–112]

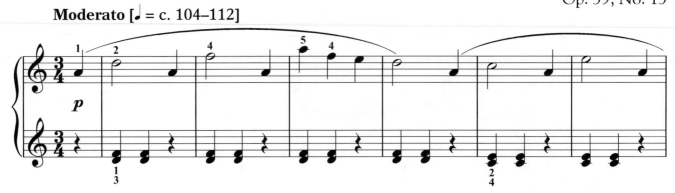

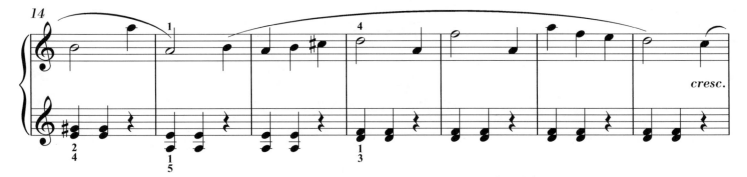

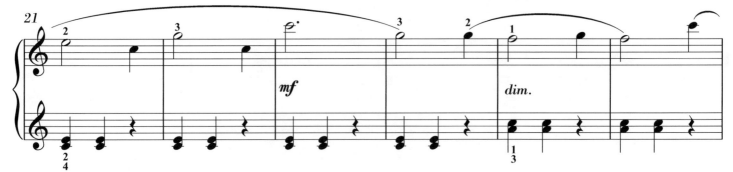

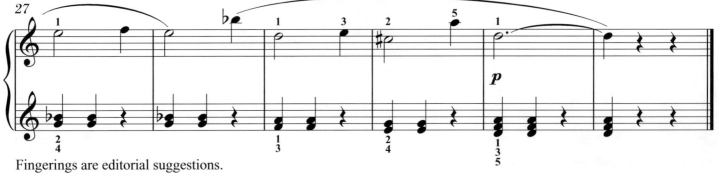

Fingerings are editorial suggestions.

Minuet
from Sonatina in C Major

Charles Henry Wilton

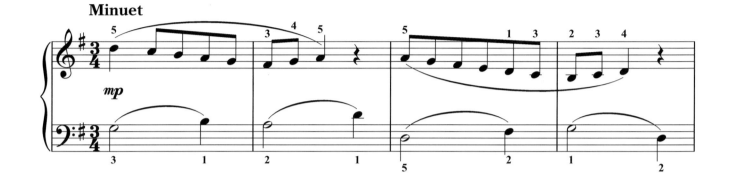

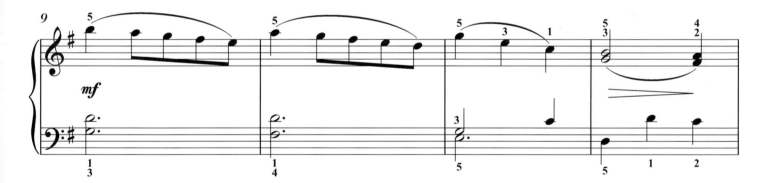

Dynamics, fingerings, and articulations are editorial suggestions.

Minuet in C Major

Wolfgang Amadeus Mozart
K. 6 (I)

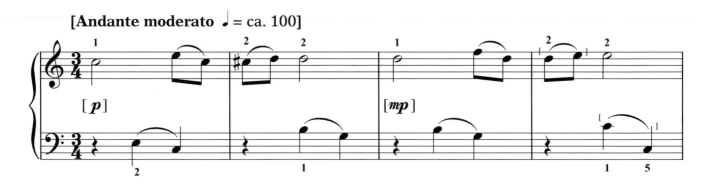

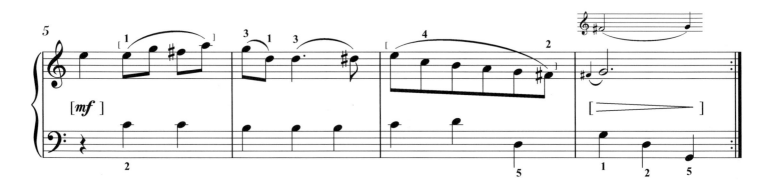

Fingerings are editorial suggestions.

The Little Harpist
from *35 Easy Pieces*

Dmitri Kabalevsky
Op. 89, No. 24

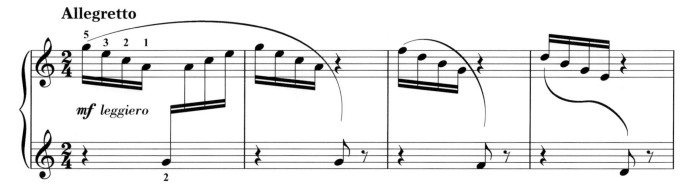

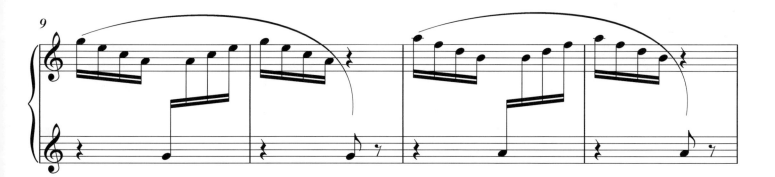

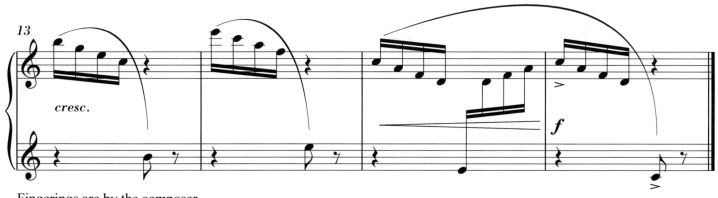

Fingerings are by the composer.

Walking
from *The First Term at the Piano*

Belá Bartók

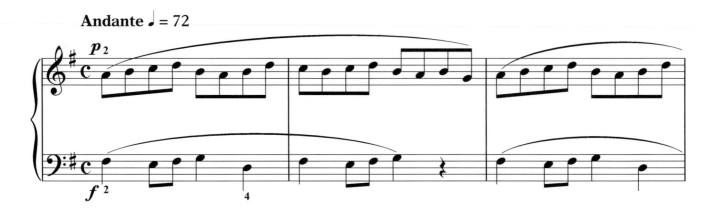

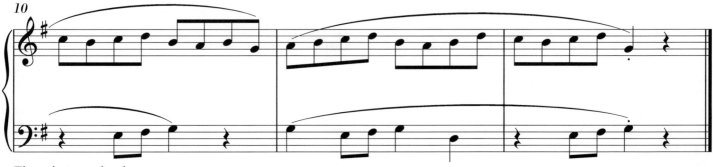

Fingerings are by the composer.

Stubborn Little Brother
from *35 Easy Pieces*

Dmitri Kabalevsky
Op. 89, No. 27

Fingerings are by the composer.
*Use fingers 2 and 3.

Pease-Porridge Hot

from *Eight Piano Pieces*

David Diamond

Fingerings are by the composer.

Air on the G String
from Orchestral Suite No. 3 in D Major

Johann Sebastian Bach
arranged by Richard Walters
BWV 1068

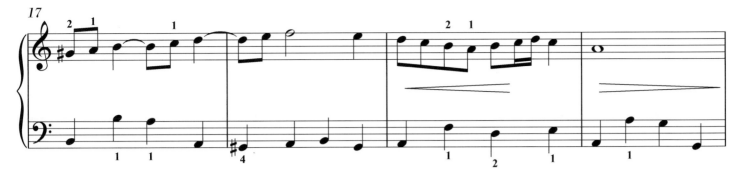

The Chase

William Duncombe

Allegro [♩ = c. 80]

Fingerings, tempo, and dynamics are editorial suggestions.

Little Goat Limping

from *35 Easy Pieces*

Dmitri Kabalevsky
Op. 89, No. 19

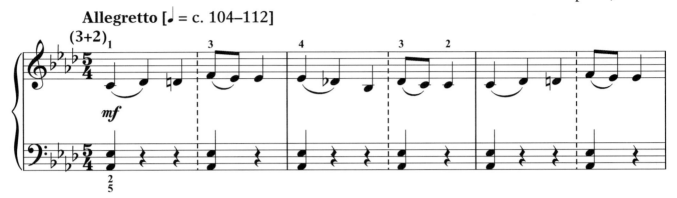

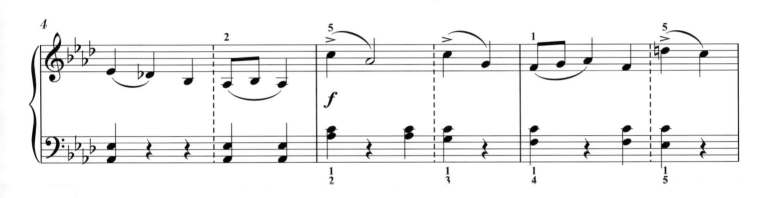

Fingerings are by the composer.

Amabile
from Sonatina in C Major

Charles Henry Wilton

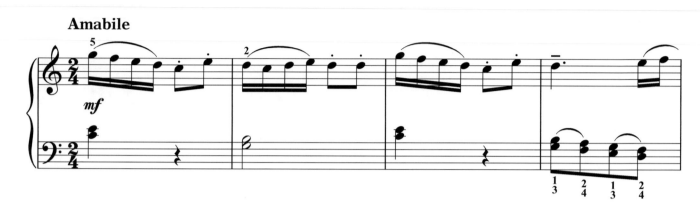

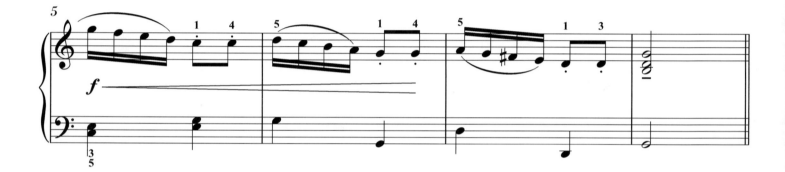

Fingerings and articulations are editorial suggestions.

Air in A-flat Major

Wolfgang Amadeus Mozart
K. Anh. 109b, Nr. 8 (15ff)

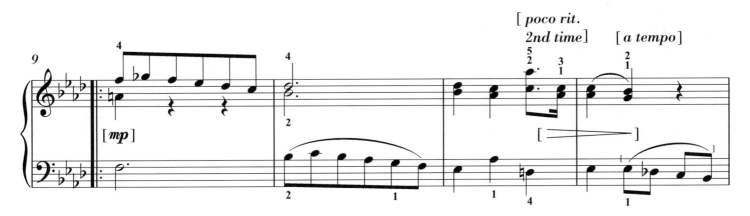

Fingerings are editorial suggestions.

Minuet in B-flat Major

Wolfgang Amadeus Mozart
K. 15pp

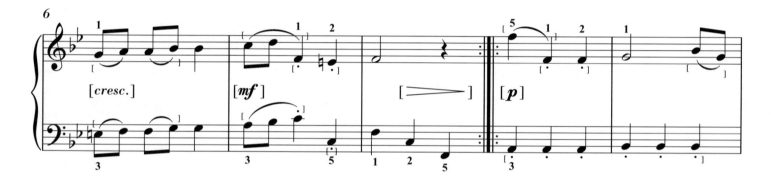

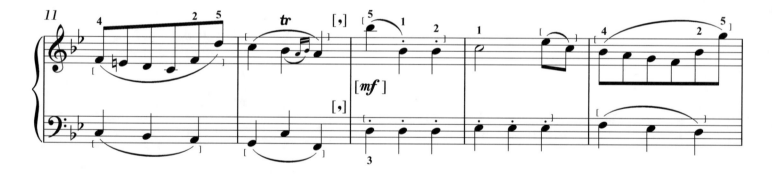

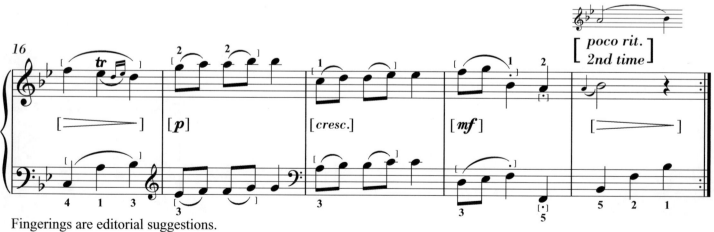

Fingerings are editorial suggestions.

Ecossaise in G Major

Ludwig van Beethoven
WoO 23
transcribed by Carl Czerny

Fingerings are editorial suggestions.

The Bear
from *Children's Notebook for Piano*

Dmitri Shostakovich
Op. 69, No. 3

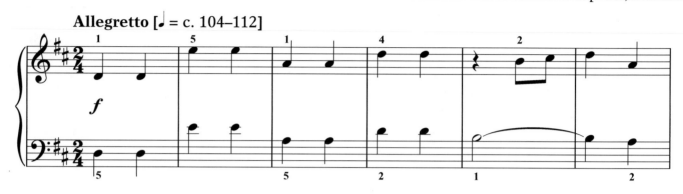

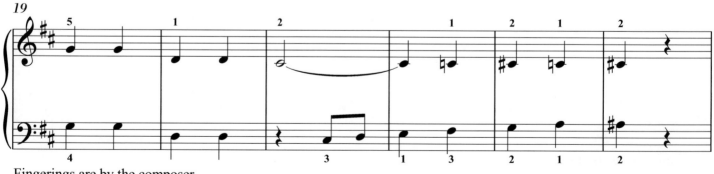

Fingerings are by the composer.

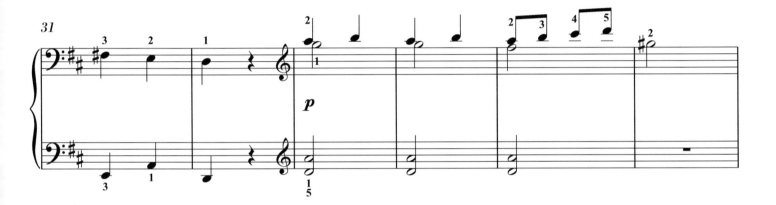

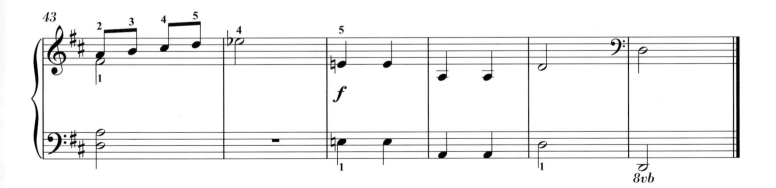

Loud and Soft
from *Ten for Deborah*

Morton Gould

Brightly [♩ = c. 180–200]

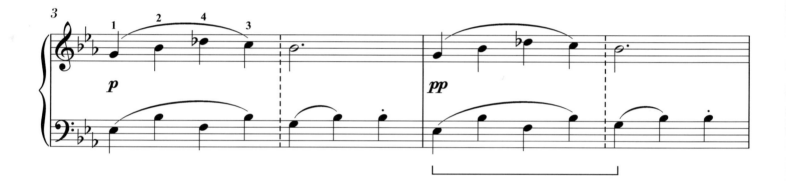

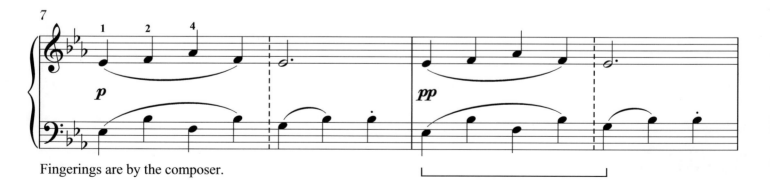

Fingerings are by the composer.

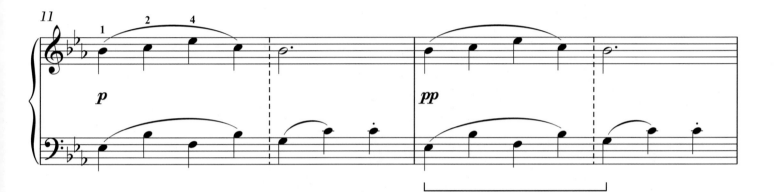

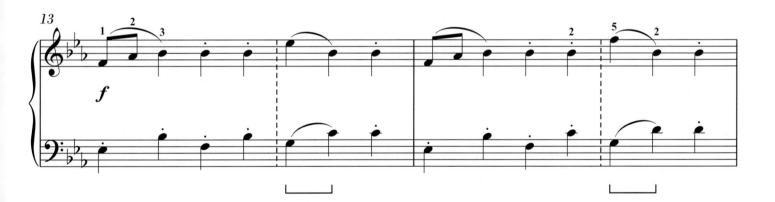

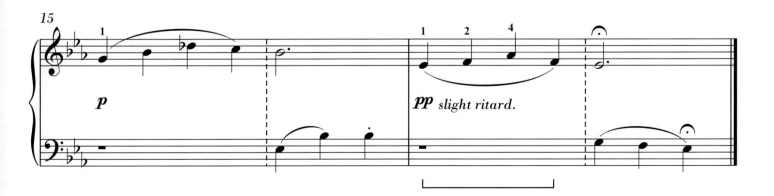

Morning Prayer
(Morgengebet)
from *Albumleaves for the Young*

Cornelius Gurlitt
Op. 101, No. 2

Adagio

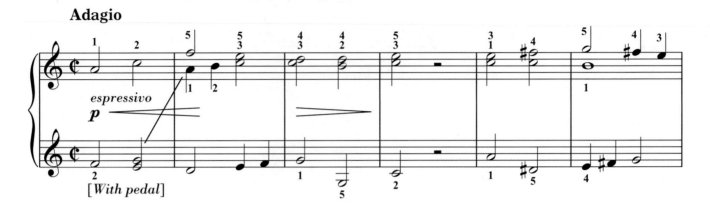

espressivo

[With pedal]

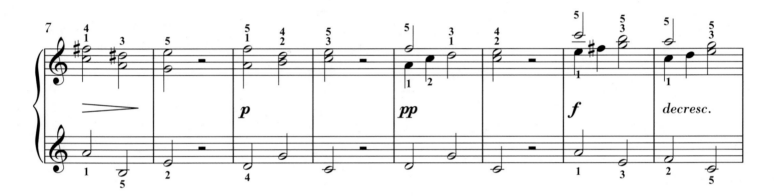

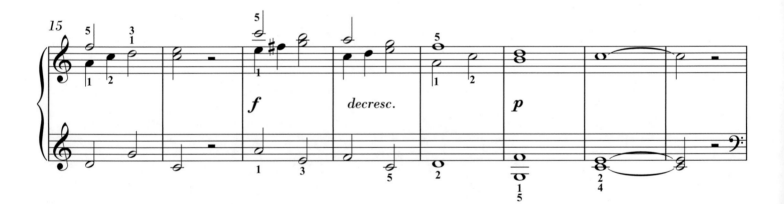

Fingerings are editorial suggestions.

Soldiers' March
(Soldatenmarsch)
from *Album for the Young*

Robert Schumann
Op. 68, No. 2

Munter und straff
Lively and strict

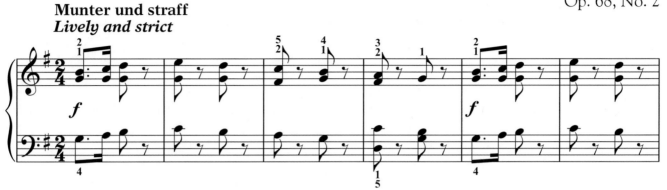

Fingerings are editorial suggestions.

Sad Tale
from *Children's Notebook for Piano*

Dmitri Shostakovich
Op. 69, No. 5

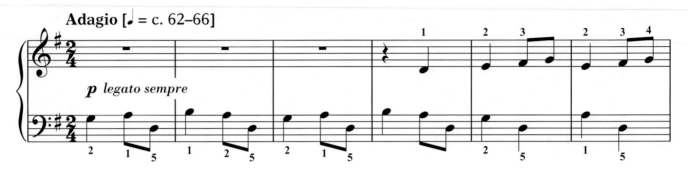

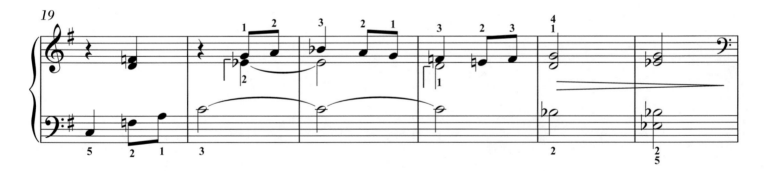

Fingerings are by the composer.

[*L.H. crosses over*]

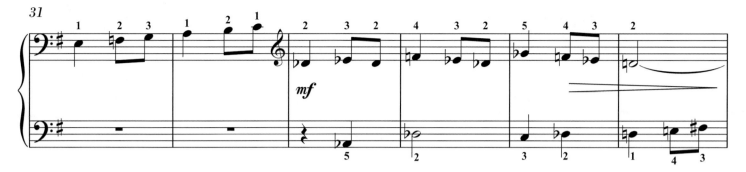

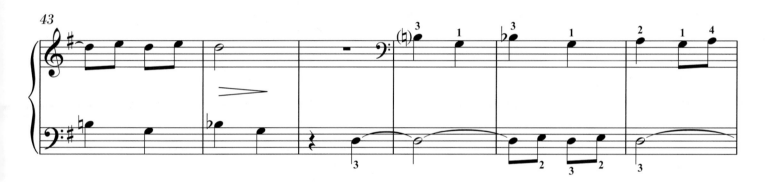

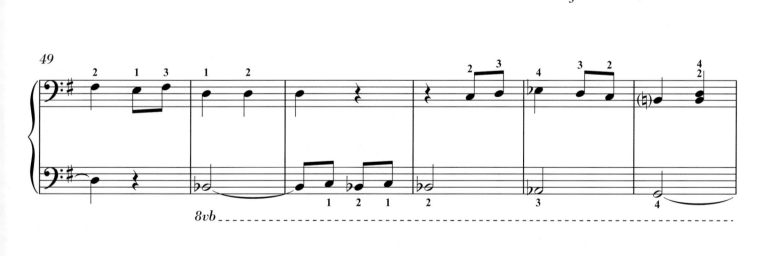

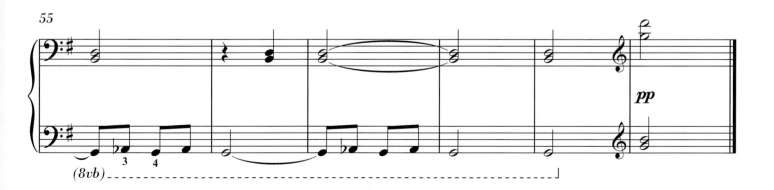

Arabesque
(L'arabesque)
from *25 Easy and Progressive Studies*

Johann Friedrich Burgmüller
Op. 100, No. 2

Allegro scherzando (♩ = 152)

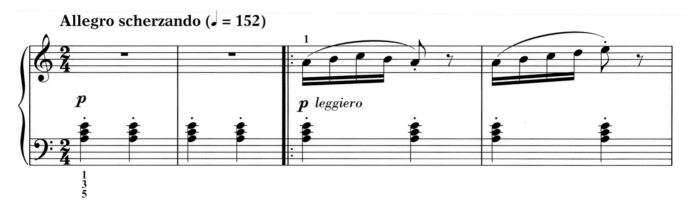

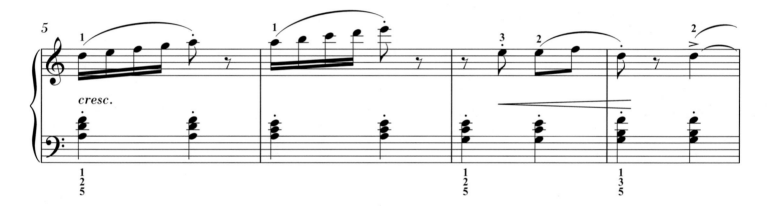

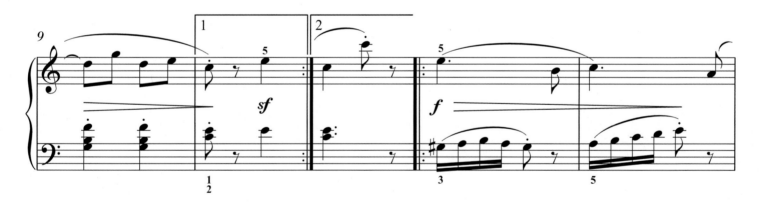

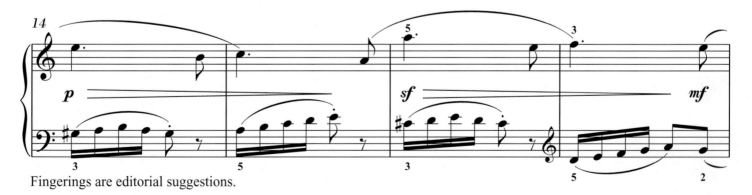

Fingerings are editorial suggestions.

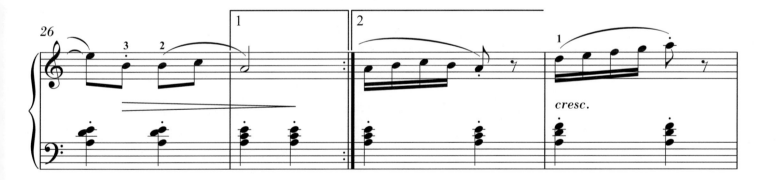

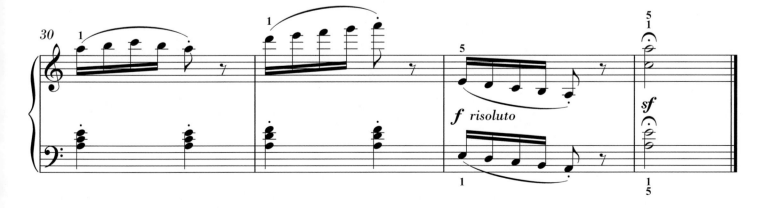

Merry Tale
from *Children's Notebook for Piano*

Dmitri Shostakovich
Op. 69, No. 4

Fingerings are by the composer.

Meow! Purr!
(Miaou! Ronron!)
from *Album pour les tout-petits*

Mélanie Bonis
Op. 103, No. 15

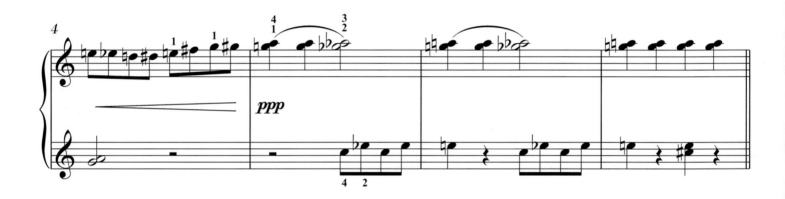

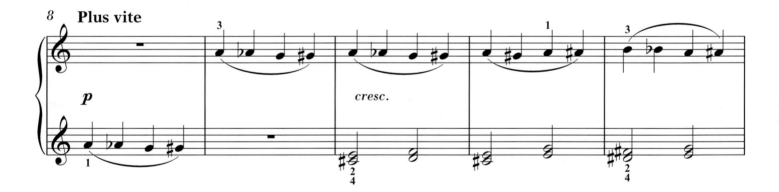

Fingerings are by the composer.

The Shrew
from *35 Easy Pieces*

Dmitri Kabalevsky
Op. 89, No. 12

Allegro marcato [♩ = c. 120–132]

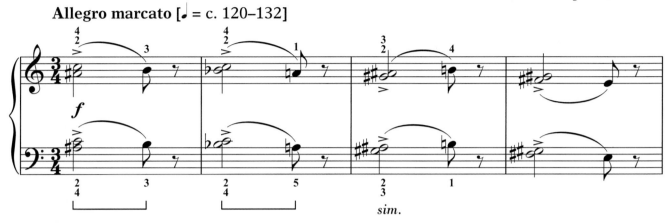

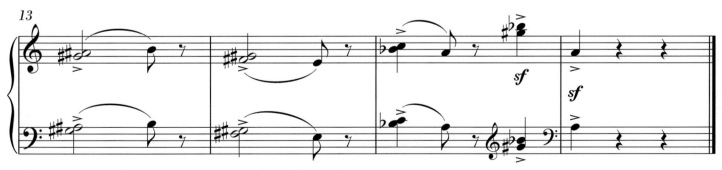

The composer deliberately uses enharmonic spellings of notes.
Fingerings are by the composer.

Melody
(Melodie)
from *Album for the Young*

Robert Schumann
Op. 68, No. 1

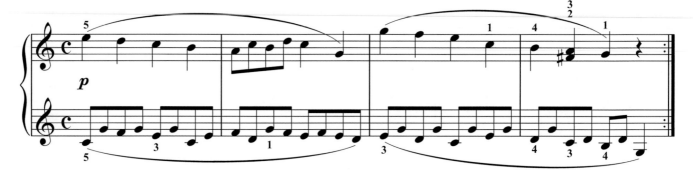

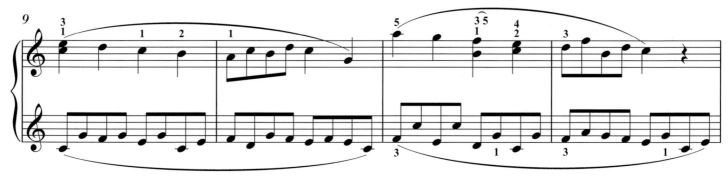

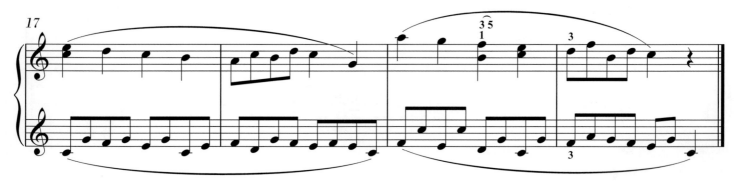

Clowns
from *24 Pieces for Children*

Dmitri Kabalevsky
Op. 39, No. 20

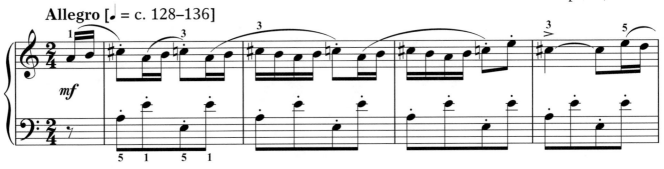

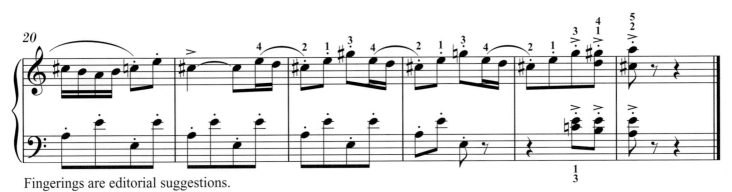

Fingerings are editorial suggestions.

The Sewing Machine
(La machine a coudre)
from *Album pour les tout-petits*

Mélanie Bonis
Op. 103, No. 6

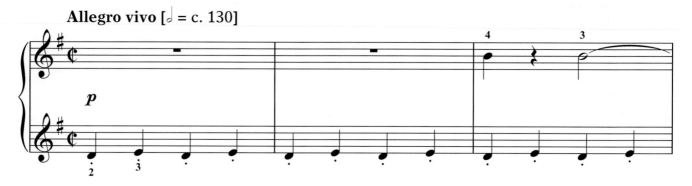

Fingerings are by the composer.

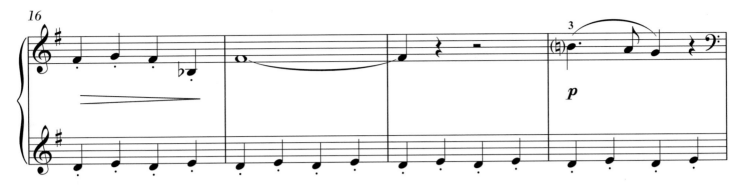

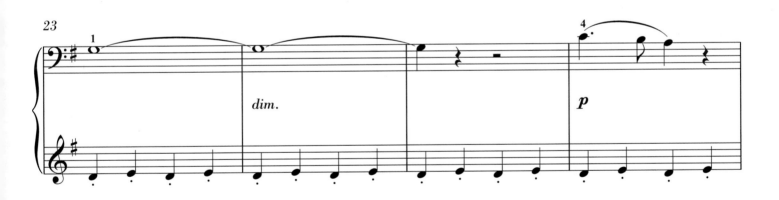